B(

Eat Like a Local- Sarasota: Sarasota Florida Food Guide

I have lived in the Sarasota area since 1998 and learned about many great places that I want to try. –Conoal

EAT LIKE A LOCAL-CONNECTICUT: Connecticut Food Guide

This a great guide to try different places in Connecticut to eat. Can't wait to try them all! The author is awesome to explore and try all these different foods/drinks. There are places I didn't know they existed until I got this book and I am a CT resident myself! –Caroline J. H.

EAT LIKE A LOCAL- LAS VEGAS: Las Vegas Nevada Food Guide

Perfect food guide for any tourist traveling to Vegas or any local looking to go outside their comfort zone! –TheBondes

Eat Like a Local-Jacksonville: Jacksonville Florida Food Guide

Loved the recommendations. Great book from someone who knows their way around Jacksonville. –Anonymous

EAT LIKE A LOCAL- COSTA BRAVA: Costa Brava Spain Food Guide

The book was very well written. Visited a few of the restaurants in the book, they were great! Sylvia V.

Eat Like a Local-Sacramento: Sacramento California Food Guide

As a native of Sacramento, Emerald's book touches on some of our areas premier spots for food and fun. She skims the surface of what Sacramento has to offer recommending locations in historical, popular areas where even more jewels can be found. –Katherine G.

EAT LIKE A LOCAL- GENEVA

Geneva Switzerland Food Guide

Emily Winters

CZYK Publishing Since 2011.
CZYKPublishing.com
Eat Like a Local

Lock Haven, PA
All rights reserved.
ISBN: 9798481027708

BOOK DESCRIPTION

Are you excited about planning your next trip? Do you want an edible experience? Would you like some culinary guidance from a local? If you answered yes to any of these questions, then this Eat Like a Local book is for you. Eat Like a Local - Geneva by Emily Winters offers the inside scoop on food in Geneva. Culinary tourism is an important aspect of any travel experience. Food has the ability to tell you a story of a destination, its landscapes, and culture on a single plate. Most food guides tell you how to eat like a tourist. Although there is nothing wrong with that, as part of the Eat Like a Local series, this book will give you a food guide from someone who has lived at your next culinary destination.

In these pages, you will discover advice on having a unique edible experience. This book will not tell you exact addresses or hours but instead will give you excitement and knowledge of food and drinks from a local that you may not find in other travel food guides.

Eat like a local. Slow down, stay in one place, and get to know the food, people, and culture. By the time you finish this book, you will be eager and prepared to travel to your next culinary destination.

OUR STORY

Traveling has always been a passion of the creator of the Eat Like a Local book series. During Lisa's travels in Malta, instead of tasting what the city offered, she ate at a large fast-food chain. However, she realized that her traveling experience would have been more fulfilling if she had experienced the best of local cuisines. Most would agree that food is one of the most important aspects of a culture. Through her travels, Lisa learned how much locals had to share with tourists, especially about food. Lisa created the Eat Like a Local book series to help connect people with locals which she discovered is a topic that locals are very passionate about sharing. So please join me and: Eat, drink, and explore like a local.

TABLE OF CONTENTS

DEDICATION

This book is dedicated to my boyfriend. Thank you for all the adventures.

ABOUT THE AUTHOR

Emily Winters is an author and English teacher who lives in Geneva, Switzerland. Emily loves to write, eat, and especially to write about eating. After living in Geneva for four years, she likes to consider herself a local, although she still finds many new restaurants and foods try.

HOW TO USE THIS BOOK

The goal of this book is to help culinary travelers either dream or experience different edible experiences by providing opinions from a local. The author has made suggestions based on their own knowledge. Please do your own research before traveling to the area in case the suggested locations are unavailable.

Travel Advisories: As a first step in planning any trip abroad, check the Travel Advisories for your intended destination.
https://travel.state.gov/content/travel/en/traveladvisories/traveladvisories.html

FROM THE PUBLISHER

Traveling can be one of the most important parts of a person's life. The anticipation and memories that you have are some of the best. As a publisher of the *Eat Like a Local*, Greater Than a Tourist, as well as the popular *50 Things to Know* book series, we strive to help you learn about new places, spark your imagination, and inspire you. Wherever you are and whatever you do I wish you safe, fun, and inspiring travel.

Lisa Rusczyk Ed. D.
CZYK Publishing

"All you need is love. But a little chocolate now and then doesn't hurt."

– Charles M. Schulz

S o, you're thinking about visiting Geneva? Let me just say, you should! If my time in Geneva has taught me anything, it's that this city will never stop surprising you, or feeding you. I have had some of the best experiences of my life, both culinary and otherwise, in Geneva, and I truly believe that the same will happen for most people who come here. Do you like delicious, one-of-a-kind chocolates? Geneva is the city for you. Do you like fine dining with sweeping views over a shining lake and towering Alps? Geneva is for you. Do you like hot, delicious, cheesy pizza? Geneva is for you, too. Alright, alright, I'll stop trying to sell you on the city (for now). Let's jump right in to the 50 things you need to know about eating like a local in Geneva.

Geneva
Switzerland

Geneva Switzerland Climate

	High	Low
January	40	29
February	44	30
March	52	34
April	59	40
May	67	47
June	74	53
July	79	57
August	78	56
September	70	50
October	59	44
November	48	36
December	41	31

GreaterThanaTourist.com

Temperatures are in Fahrenheit degrees.
Source: NOAA

1. GENEVOISE FOOD: AN UNFORGETTABLE EXPERIENCE

For me, Geneva will always be a city of food. From the first day I arrived, I have hardly had any bad food experiences – which is pretty crazy, because anyone who has ever met me will tell you that I am an incredibly picky eater. Some days are about a flaky chocolate croissant from the patisserie next to my apartment. Other days are about a fine candle-lit dinner in a restaurant far grander on the inside than the outside. From a piece of milk chocolate in shiny wrapping left on your hotel room pillow to a plate of crunchy-soft roesti, Geneva always has a new twist on a Swiss classic.

Now, you might be thinking that I'm a little biased. As someone who lives in Geneva (and loves chocolate more than just about anything) it would be easy for me to get too excited about the options here. I promise you, though, that Genevoise food really does live up to the hype. Every one of my friends and family who have visited me there end their visit with the same review: the food here is unforgettable.

2. A MEAL FOR EVERYONE

As I mentioned before, I am quite picky. I have been a vegetarian for most of my life and tend to shy away from a few other foods for no particular reason (don't you dare threaten me with a zucchini, for instance). My boyfriend is equally picky, but in a very different way. He loves meat, especially chicken, is petrified of tomatoes, and enjoys making fun of vegetarian food (and vegetarian people and vegetarian restaurants). The list goes on: nearly all of my friends have more than a few foods that they refuse to eat, and the foods they do like hardly ever overlap. Yet in Geneva, we can almost always find a restaurant that we all like. From my favorite falafel shop, which also sells excellent kebabs, to pizza restaurants with more toppings than stars in the sky, to Swiss restaurants famous for both meat and vegetables, Genevoise restaurants really do have something for everyone. Are you getting hungry yet? I sure am. But before you start reserving your tables, let's talk about timing.

3. WHEN TO VISIT

One of the best things about Geneva, other than the food, is the fact that every season has something to recommend it. I usually hate spring, but in Geneva I can't help falling in love with the budding trees, light rain, and seasonal produce in the local farmer's markets. Summer brings warmer weather, although Geneva is rarely too hot, along with swims in the lake and small pop-up ice cream carts on every sidewalk. Fall is full of changing leaves, cool breezes, and the ice cream carts switching out their freezers for enormous cauldrons of roasted chestnuts. Finally, winter brings Christmas, the occasional flurry of snow, and delicious Christmas cookies in a dizzying array of shapes, sizes, and flavors. In the end, the season I recommend for a first visit is the season I love the most anyway: fall. Fall in Geneva is usually crisp and cool, drawing tourists and locals alike out into the streets for long walks and into small cafes for cups of hot chocolate, strong coffee, and sweet pastries. Just watch out for Sundays, when most shops and some restaurants are closed.

4. SWISS FOOD CULTURE

The Swiss food culture is not all that different from what you might find in another Western country, with a few differences. The Swiss generally eat a small breakfast, which is often savory. Many Swiss people enjoy bread with assorted cheeses and meats in the morning, making this a popular spread in hotels as well as local's kitchens. Other people will choose a bowl of muesli, which is a crunchy cereal usually made with oatmeal, dried fruits and nuts, and sometimes bits of chocolate covered with fresh milk.

Lunch is a more formal affair often enjoyed with colleagues or classmates. Some Swiss will choose to have lighter fair at this time, such as salads and sandwiches. Others see lunch as their main meal and will seek out something heartier, ranging from traditional Swiss sausages and potatoes to Italian pasta or Indian curries. In restaurants, lunch can often be ordered from a special lunch menu, which has lower prices, smaller portions, and a slightly reduced selection.

Dinner is usually enjoyed at home with the family. Some Swiss people will take this opportunity to enjoy a more complicated meal, but, as in any country, dinner can also be leftovers or a dish thrown together from whichever vegetables looked best in the supermarket that day. In a restaurant, dinner is usually more formal and can be ordered from the full menu, which will generally include starters, main courses, and desserts. Next, let's talk a little about what to expect when you go to pay.

5. TIPPING AND TAX

It can be more than a little stressful to arrive at a restaurant in a foreign country without knowing how tipping should be handled. Luckily, tipping is quite straightforward in Swiss restaurants and won't be much of a surprise to travelers from the United States or Europe. It is generally polite to leave a small tip, usually about 15%. Customers will often simply round the bill up when paying to include the tip or will leave a few small coins or bills on the table (although this is a bit less common). Of course, small kebab shops, ice cream stands, and pizza places generally don't expect a tip, although they will be pleased if you drop a few coins into the tip jar usually found on their counters.

Taxes are also an important, if slightly less exciting, part of eating out. Luckily, Geneva rarely has surprises as far as price goes. A small VAT tax is added to most purchases at 2.5% for most everyday items, including food in restaurants, groceries, and books and magazines. Hotel stays, including breakfasts in hotels, are taxed at 3.7%. Finally, clothes, most services, and alcohol is taxed at the highest rate of 7.7%. Many restaurants will take VAT into account on their menu prices to avoid problematic surprises, but be sure to check this when you are browsing the menu. How can you pay for your delicious meal (and tax and tip)? We'll talk about that next.

6. WAYS TO PAY

Geneva is an easy city for payment, because almost every restaurant will take cards, including cards from abroad. There may be a slight conversion cost of a few extra percent if you pay with a card from another country, but it is usually not too high. Check with your card provider for exact information about the conversion fees. Both debit and credit cards are accepted almost everywhere, including in small restaurants and stores. In very few cases you will need to pay with cash, but the restaurant will usually indicate this with a sign.

When you do pay in cash, the best option is to pay with Swiss Francs (CHF). Although many restaurants also accept Euros, the conversion fee for this is usually quite high. Francs come in bills ranging from ten to one thousand francs and coins ranging from five "centimes" to five francs. Don't worry if the ATM spits out a wad of large bills: this is very common in Geneva, and most restaurants (and stores) will happily accept even 200 franc bills. A few restaurants also accept Google Pay or Apple Pay, although it is best not to count on this.

Now let's move on to the fun part: the actual restaurants and food you can expect to eat in Geneva.

7. ROMANTIC DATE-NIGHT RESTAURANTS

My first date with my current boyfriend almost went very badly. We met in Peillonex, a peripheral region of Geneva popular with students and retirees for its lower prices and more pastoral atmosphere. After exchanging the traditional Swiss cheek kisses (three in total), he led me towards what looked like the tiniest restaurant I had ever seen. I was a bit concerned as we climbed the rickety stairs, but when we opened the door and swept aside a small curtain, we were in one of the loveliest restaurants I'd ever seen. The wait staff was amazing, the food was delicious, offering both vegetarian and meat options and a truly amazing apple-cinnamon-ice cream dessert that I have still not forgotten two years later. It was Italian at its freshest. So, whether you're on a first date or a hundred and first date, I would strongly recommend Mapo. The prices are a bit high, but the food is worth it. Reservations are recommended, although they usually have tables available on the same day.

For a more exotic date experience, Parsargades offers delicious Iranian food, beautiful chandeliers, and friendly English-speaking wait staff. Café Zinette also offers fresh, often local, food options, a variety of drinks, and a spectacular terrace to enjoy in the warmer months.

Got some little ones who might not enjoy a fine glass of Cabernet? Don't worry, next we'll dive in to some of Geneva's most kid-friendly establishments.

8. KID-FRIENDLY FEASTS

Geneva is surprisingly kid-friendly overall. Many restaurants have children's menus, and even in more upscale establishments customers generally turn a polite smile on a messy toddler. Sometimes, though, it's nice to eat in a place where kids are not just accepted but welcomed. Wolfisberg, a café in Carouge, is one of those places. With an indoor play area for rainy days and delicious pastries that will appeal to young ones (and the rest of us, too), Wolfisberg is my go-to spot when kids come to visit. When the sun is shining, Aero Bistro offers both Thai and Swiss food with a comprehensive kid's menu, an outdoor play area, and a great view of airplanes taking off and landing at Geneva airport for your more aviation-obsessed little ones. Rain or shine, Restaurant de la Plage du Reposoir overlooks the famous Jet d'Eau in Lake Geneva and offers a play corner with books, toys, and a small climbing frame for young guests. The restaurant is also quite close to the lake beach and a larger outdoor climbing structure for kids to blow off some steam after eating. Perhaps best of all, the restaurant offers a vacation-like atmosphere for kids and adults alike.

Sometimes, though, the best food for kids is something quick, inexpensive, and delicious, which is what we'll discuss next.

9. DELICIOUSNESS ON A BUDGET

Even on vacation, not every meal can be an expensive eight-course extravaganza. For locals, this is even more important. That's probably why, although it is a notoriously expensive city, Geneva does offer quite a few options for affordable meals. One of the best options is Parfums de Beyrouth, a Lebanese restaurant located near the main train station. Parfums de Beyrouth is my first choice restaurant when meeting friends, when large groups come to visit, and simply when I'm hungry and need a quick, cheap bite. They have fresh falafel wraps and plates, both chicken and beef shawarma, and an assortment of tasty side dishes. After ordering at the counter, you can find a table in the restaurant or, on sunny days, take your order to go and have an impromptu picnic along the nearby lake.

Another excellent option for inexpensive food is Café Restaurant Cite-Jardin, a pizza place located in the atrium of one of the University of Geneva's dorms. Although the restaurant is mostly known among students for its low prices, the pizza is actually amazing: saucy, cheesy, hot, covered in all the toppings you could want, and ready fast. The restaurant is surrounded by glass windows overlooking a green area, making it a nice place to sit and eat. When things get a bit busy, the restaurant will often give a free ice tea to customers who order pizza to go; if you choose this option, you can enjoy your pizza and tea in any one of the many local parks.

Inexpensive food is often easy to spot: Indian food served out of the window of a ground floor apartment, a hot dog cart on the shore of Lake Geneva, and just about any falafel place come to mind. What's more surprising, though, is that even cheap food in Geneva tends to be delicious. Watch out for fast food restaurants, like McDonald's, though: despite the fact that they are usually cheap in other countries, international fast food chains tend to be a bit expensive in Geneva.

Sometimes, expensive can be worth it. After all, if you aren't going to splurge on vacation, when will you? That's why the next section discusses a few Geneva restaurants that run on the pricier side, but that are worth every franc.

10. DELICIOUSNESS ON A (HIGHER) BUDGET

Geneva is known for fine dining. With beautiful dining rooms, seasonal produce, and fusions of different cuisines, what's not to love about upscale Genevoise dining? Eastwest Hotel offers exactly that. Serving traditional Swiss dishes with an Eastern flare, Eastwest Hotel is a fantastic restaurant worthy of a visit. The décor is dark and refined, with a small outdoor terrace available in the summer months.

Il Lago is another outstanding restaurant. With delectable Italian/Mediterranean fusion dishes, a lavish dining room, and a well-deserved Michelin star, Il Lago is internationally renowned and certainly worth a splurge.

Finally, Les Armures, known as one of the oldest restaurants in the city, offers an elegant yet relaxing atmosphere and a range of French and Swiss specialties, including fondue and raclette (which I'll discuss more later). This is one of the best places to sample fresh, delicious Swiss cuisine in a refined environment and is one of my top recommendations.

In short, if you're in the mood for something delicious, fresh, and local, Geneva has options for you!

11. PHOTOGENIC FOOD

Taste is everything, right? Well, not quite. If you've ever been sitting in a restaurant, seen your food come out of the kitchen, and be unable to believe your eyes, you know exactly what I'm talking about. Instagram-worthy dishes can be great fun. By far the most photogenic food in Geneva can be found at Black Tap, a burgers-and-milkshakes restaurant known for their crazy creations. One milkshake is plenty for two people and makes for some pretty awesome photos, if you can keep from digging in long enough to snap a few. Their Cake Shake, which comes with a large slice of cake balanced on the rim of the glass, is a standout, but my personal favorite is the Sweet and Salty shake, which is packed with peanut butter, chocolate, pretzels, and creamy goodness. It is probably best that I don't tell you how often I have stopped by Black Tap for a shake. Their burgers are also delicious and make for good photos.

Of course, spectacular food isn't the only photogenic thing to seek out: excellent views can also make a meal amazing.

12. BEST VIEWS

In Geneva, the best views usually involve Lake Geneva. A sprawling, clear, shining expanse known as Lac Leman by the locals, Lake Geneva makes for some breathtaking photo spots. La Perle du Lac, an Italian restaurant that draws on local flavors and produce, offers an unparalleled view, especially at sunset. Parc des Eaux Vives also has a small restaurant with a gracefully slopping roof that highlights seasonal flavors and boasts a large outdoor patio with great lake views. The only problem with the lake-view restaurants, though, is that along with the expansive views and delicious dishes usually comes a large price tag. To get around this, I recommend making your own lovely view with a personalized picnic.

13. PERFECT PICNICS

One of my fondest memories of summer in Geneva is sitting with a friend in Jardin Anglais, a large English-style garden situation directly on the banks of Lake Geneva. It was a hot and sunny day and we had commandeered a bench just a stone's throw from the water. Between us was a large loaf of crusty French bread, a wedge of fragrant cheese, a small box of raspberries, a bar of chocolate, and a bottle of ginger lemonade. All had been purchased from the local grocery store for next to nothing and all were absolutely delicious. After eating we strolled along the lake front, chatting, and bought an ice cream from a small stand as we passed. It was an almost perfect day.

Jardin Anglais is certainly one of the best picnic spots in Geneva, although it is far from the only one. Geneve-Plage, a beach with a large playground and room for swimming, is located just a bit further along the shore and offers numerous beautiful picnic spots. On the other side of the lake, the Bains des Paquis boardwalk juts out into the lake, culminating in a lighthouse. As well as a swimming area and fondue restaurant, Bains des Paquis has several lovely spots to sit, eat, and enjoy the view. Don't let the small gate at the beginning of the boardwalk fool you: it is free to enter.

For your picnic cuisine, I recommend doing what I have done countless times: go in to your local grocery store, have a look around, and pick out a few breads and cheeses. It is cheap, delicious, and lets you experience a bit of local flavor that you might not find in a restaurant.

14. GROCERY SHOPPING

Whether you are picking up a light lunch for your picnic, finding a few snacks for your hotel room, or just looking around, Genevoise grocery stores are worth a visit (or two). It's fun to see what the locals like to eat and you will occasionally stumble upon something truly delicious (or just plain interesting) that you wouldn't have seen otherwise. For inexpensive shopping, stop by your local Denner, Lidl, or Aldi. All three are German grocery stores that offer local ingredients at a lower cost. For a bit more quality, try Coop or Migros, two Swiss supermarket chains stocked with everything from fresh fruit to taco kits.

Any large supermarket will have more or less anything you want, including some pre-packaged meals for a quick and cheap food option. The packaged sandwiches are surprisingly tasty. Supermarkets can also be an excellent place for breakfast, as I will explain later. Genevoise supermarkets are currently campaigning for reusable bags, so if you have a small tote for your groceries, make sure to bring it. If you don't, don't worry: you can also purchase a paper bag for just a few cents. You can easily pay with card or cash at any major supermarket, although a few of the smallest convenience stores will be cash-only. Watch out for a small sign next to the cash register to warn you in this case.

One excellent thing about Swiss grocery stores is that they allow you to do a bit of cooking yourself on your visit, if you decide to do so.

15. HOTEL ROOM COOKING

There are some nights when you just don't want to go out, even on vacation. Maybe you want to save a bit of money; maybe you are just tired and want to lay on your bed and catch up on a TV show while you eat. These are the days when you might consider a little hotel room cooking.

Swiss supermarkets can help you here. From soups that just require hot water to frozen meals that can be heated up in a microwave to sandwiches and salads that require nothing at all, supermarkets offer a range of packaged foods for your convenience. If you're staying in an Airbnb with a kitchen, you can get even more creative. As well as fresh ingredients for cooking from scratch, Coop offers things like taco kits and bags of roesti that can be heated in a pan.

Have a look: you may be surprised by how much food you can cook in a hotel room or Airbnb, and by how good it tastes.

Sometimes, though, you just don't feel like eating microwave meals or like going out to dinner. In these cases, I would recommend using one of Geneva's take-out services.

16. TAKE-OUT AND DELIVERY

Most restaurants, especially pizza or kebab restaurants, will offer take-out. Just go to their website – you will usually find an "order" button at the top. Often they will ask you to pick up the order, though, so make sure that you are choosing a restaurant close by or that they will deliver to you instead.

For delivery, the best option is the Just Eat Geneva app or Uber Eats. Both are similarly priced and similarly good: the main difference is that each has different restaurants. Have a look at both and choose the one with food that appeals to you more, or choose one at random. You can expect to pay a small delivery fee based on the distance to your accommodation from the restaurant and can choose to add a tip for the driver within the app. Tips through the app are encouraged over tips in person to the driver. After your order-in meal, I bet you'll be craving a bit of dessert; I usually am.

17. SWEET TREATS

I have a bit of a sweet tooth. If I'm being honest, more than a bit. That is probably the hardest thing for me about living in Geneva: I am constantly surrounded by sweet treats and I am constantly trying not to ruin my dinner by stuffing myself with said treats. The first place I have to mention is Black Tap. I know, I know, I already told you about that one, but it is so good that it is worth repeating. Did I mention the creamy milkshake with the slice of cake on top? Did I mention that they have a vegan milkshake, too? Did I tell you about the one with the giant cookie? Okay, I'll stop, but only if you promise to try Black Tap yourself.

If you're not in the mood for a milkshake (are you ever not in the mood for a milkshake?) Mueller's Factory is another perfect option. They serve both sweet and savory crepes and waffles, although of course I recommend the sweet. The crepe with caramel sauce and vanilla ice cream is absolutely to die for and the view from the outdoor tables onto old buildings and a small park makes for a great atmosphere.

Sometimes the best sweet treat, though, is the one you stumble across in the local patisserie, or sweet bakery. They are on almost every street in Geneva and offer a range of pastries.

18. NAVIGATING A PATISSERIE

Patisseries are one of the best parts of Geneva. The glass cases inside brim with different baked goods, from slices of raspberry cake covered with rich frosting to fluffy rolls studded with chocolate pieces to wobbly, crusty crème brulees, there is truly something for every craving. It can be a little stressful to enter your first patisserie, especially if you don't speak French, but have no fear. Most pastries can be identified visually, so you will be able to pick out something delicious even without reading the placards. Most people speak English well, so feel free to ask the person behind the counter questions in English or to simply point to what you want if you can't pronounce the name. It is best to have some cash on hand, as some patisseries, especially the small ones, prefer to accept payment in cash. Make sure to order a few treats, as they are usually small and far too delicious to be satisfied with just one.

19. FABULOUSLY FROZEN

You may have noticed that I didn't mention ice cream as a sweet treat. Don't worry, it isn't because I'm some crazy ice-cream hater: I just thought that ice cream deserves its own section. Don't you agree?

The best gelato in Geneva can be found at Manu Gelato or Gelatomania, two local chains with a few locations around Geneva. Both serve a wide range of freshly-made flavors and both are staffed by friendly locals who are always happy to give samples, recommend a new flavor, or let you practice a little French.

In the summer, the best ice cream can be found at the local pop-up stands along the lake. As the temperatures climb, more and more small carts open. Choose a local stand if possible, as opposed to a Haagen-Dazs stand: the local ones are usually cheaper, more delicious, and let you support a local business. Just start a stroll along the lakefront, or even along one of the rivers feeding into the lake, and you are sure to stumble across something cold, creamy, and unforgettable. Make sure to enjoy your treat early in the day as most stands close before dark.

20. LATE NIGHT BITES

Geneva is not the biggest city for night life, if I'm being honest with you. Sure, you can find a nice bar or pub at any hour, but if you're looking for a full meal, you'll have to look a little harder. Most restaurants close around 9:00pm, sometimes even earlier, so if you're craving a midnight snack, you may have to get creative. Sundays can also be a little tricky, as some restaurants will close along with the stores.

Have no fear, though. Nighttime is when I recommend turning to kebabs, of which the best is Parfums du Beyrouth (as I mentioned earlier). If you're not in the area, you can still find a good kebab shop on almost any street: the skewers of slowly rotating meats and the smell of French fries always give them away. Try a kebab box if you are looking for something a little more filling.

If you're not in the mood for kebabs, try the train station. There the restaurants and shops are open a bit later and on Sundays as well. The usually serve decent food, especially if you're craving something greasy and fried.

21. UNIQUE CULINARY EXPERIENCES

Traveling is an excellent time to eat food that you never expected, in a setting that you couldn't have predicted. Geneva has a few stand out opportunities for fine dining. First, try Black Tap. Then, when you're really sick of milkshakes (or at least of hearing me talk about them) head down to the Bain des Paquis boardwalk. As you traverse the planks, you'll come to a tented restaurant down a few steps to the right. Here you can order a large pot of fondue paired with cubes of crusty bread, cuts of meat, or potatoes, as per your preference. You can also buy wines or beers as an accompaniment. The whole thing is perfect for sharing with friends and family, especially in the evening as the sun is setting along the lake and night is setting in. The whole atmosphere is full of chatter and laughter, the cheese is delicious, and the experience is unexpectedly affordable. I have more good memories than I can count of birthdays, finals, and promotions celebrated around a pot of fondue.

If you're tired of Swiss food (although I can't imagine how that would happen), take a trip around the culinary world without leaving the city at Eat Me. This unique restaurant offers a series of shareable plates that will take your taste buds on a journey through all five continents. Also, make sure to take advantage of some of Geneva's street food selections.

22. SEASONAL STREET FOOD

I already mentioned the small ice cream stands that line the shores of Lake Geneva in summer. But did I mention that, in winter, the stands turn over their signs, pack away their freezers, and start selling roasted chestnuts? Street food in Geneva is highly seasonal, with fresh fruits and ice cream sold out of tiny stalls in the summer, roasted chestnuts and caramelized almonds moving in during the autumn, and a rotating cast of food carts filling in between. These carts can usually be found in the Old Town and along Lake Geneva, or in a local farmer's market. Farmer's markets are in different locations at different times, but the market in Plainpalais (open Tuesdays, Thursdays, and Sundays) is a good bet for fresh produce and snacks from food carts. The best seasonal street food, though, comes at Christmastime.

23. CHRISTMAS MARKET DELICACIES

At the end of November, Place du Neuve, a small park just blocks away from Geneva's Old Town, is completely transformed. A skating rink is constructed, giant Christmas decorations are hung from every tree, and stalls open selling everything from socks to ornaments to amazing food. Curls of crunchy, salty potato chips covered in local herbs and skewered on long sticks are a highlight. Chimney cakes, hollow spirals of dough baked on a metal frame and coated in flavored sugar are a wonderful treat if you're in a sweeter mood. Momos, crepes, cupcakes, burgers, and tacos vie for 'most memorable treat' as well. Although the stalls open in the Christmas market do change every year, there is always something truly delicious (and there are always potato chips on sticks and chimney cakes). Here you will want to bring some cash: everything is cheap, but cards are usually not accepted. Visit the market for a late dinner and enjoy the wonderful lights, tantalizing smells, and happy chatter of Christmas market visitors of all ages.

24. CHOCOLAT: A SWISS LOVE STORY

Let me tear you away from the sights and smells of the Christmas market for a moment to talk about that most famous of Swiss foods: chocolate. Almost everyone has sampled Swiss chocolate at least once before, but Swiss chocolate in Switzerland is still better than Swiss chocolate anywhere else. After spending a few days in Geneva, you will likely have sampled a variety of chocolates, whether those are actual chocolate bars or just chocolate desserts at a patisserie. But do you know why chocolate is so important to the Swiss?

The story dates back over 200 years, when Switzerland was just an area that traders were passing through while bringing chocolate to courts in Austria and beyond. Sensing an opportunity, the Swiss began processing the chocolate, and in 1826 the first chocolate press was invented quite near Geneva.

Switzerland's rich, free-range milk also makes Swiss chocolate extra delicious, as do Swiss chocolatiers' additions of ingredients like hazelnuts. Although Switzerland has never grown a cocoa bean, its chocolate is world-renowned because of Swiss ingenuity and enterprise. Isn't it time to try a bar or two now?

25. LOST IN THE CHOCOLATE AISLE

Although you can buy delicious chocolate from small stores like Lindt and Spruengli, where they will break your chocolate selection off giant sheets and wrap it for you in sheets of clear plastic, you can also purchase delicious chocolate directly from the nearest supermarket. All supermarkets, even the smallest ones, have a large chocolate aisle filled with beautifully displayed, foil-wrapped bars. There are two main Swiss brands in contention: Callier and Lindt. Both are amazing. I would recommend purchasing a selection of bars so that you can choose your own personal favorite: both Callier and Lindt even offer multipacks with a variety of tiny chocolate bars for sampling. Swiss chocolate also makes a perfect souvenir for your family and friends back home: even grocery store chocolate is beautifully wrapped and will delight anyone who tries it.

26. A CHEESE-Y STORY

As famous as Switzerland is for chocolate, its cheese is equally well-known. Just like chocolate, you can buy quite an array of delicious cheese for any palate in your local grocery store or at a fromagerie. The best place to enjoy Swiss cheese, though, is with fondue or raclette. Fondue, as you probably know, is basically a giant pot of cheese. The cheese comes with a plate filled with ingredients to dip, usually bread, but sometimes meats, potatoes, or vegetables depending on the restaurant and on your preference. Fondue is a meal best enjoyed on a cold day with a group of friends.

Raclette, on the other hand, is usually a layer of potatoes, sometimes mixed with small cubes of ham or onion, covered with a thick layer of cheese and baked in a special oven. Although fondue is more famous, and can be a bit more fun to eat, I find raclette to be even more delicious. Almost any restaurant serving Swiss food will offer both.

27. MODERN SWISS FOOD

Along with raclette and fondue, another famous Swiss dish that you simply must try is roesti. Roesti is a bit similar to American hash browns, but thicker and crispier. To make it, potatoes are shredded, boiled, and then pan-fried in butter until both sides are golden brown and crispy. The inside remains soft and delicious, like mashed potatoes. Roesti is often served with sausages, slices of pan-fried meat, or a salad.

Another famous Swiss food worth a try is Zopf. You are likely to find it in your hotel breakfast buffet or in a local bakery. This buttery, braided bread, similar to a challah, is traditionally served on Sundays for breakfast along with meats, cheeses, butter, or jam. As you may have noticed, the Swiss really enjoy their cheese and carbs, making their food delicious, filling, and occasionally a bit unhealthy. Luckily, Geneva has plenty of international options as well.

28. INTERNATIONAL CUISINE

If you do find yourself craving a little international flair, get excited: as a diverse city with residents from around the world, Geneva has some great options for exotic food. Try Foret de bambous if you're looking for some delicious Chinese cuisine, including a particularly outstanding Szechuan eggplant dish, in a cozy settings. Sajna Restaurant has an array of Indian foods, including a lunchtime buffet, and their garlic naan never disappoints. For Latin American delights, try an empanada from Mama Wasi, a hole-in-the-wall takeout spot packed with flavor and fantastic smells. You may be noticing that the international cuisine is centered in the Cornavin area: this neighborhood is popular with expats and is on the way to the United Nations, making it particularly international. If none of the restaurants I've mentioned stand out, just take a stroll down Rue de Lausanne, the main road in this neighborhood, and you're likely to find a tasty bite from most any country.

29. NAVIGATING THE HOTEL BREAKFAST

After a day spent wandering the streets of Geneva, sampling samosas and raclette, you'll probably return to your hotel pleasantly tired and ready to sleep well and spend a slow morning perusing the hotel's breakfast spread. As I mentioned earlier, the Swiss tend to favor savory breakfasts, especially when they are eating in a hotel, so many hotels will serve crusty bread or rolls, sometimes with a croissant thrown in for good measure, along with slices of cold cuts, cheeses, tomatoes, and cucumber. You're also likely to find a few pats of butter and tea or coffee with milk and sugar. You can then assemble your own open-faced breakfast sandwich (preferably keeping the coffee or tea on the side) and enjoy it at your leisure. Some hotels will go for a sweeter option with chocolate croissants, rolls filled with Nutella, cereal, or fruit, so don't worry if you're not excited about eating sandwiches for breakfast. I will tell you that they are quite delicious, though, so don't knock the sandwich until you've tried it.

30. BREAKFAST ON A BUDGET

As delicious as hotel breakfasts can be, they are often a bit on the expensive side as well. As I mentioned before, hotel breakfasts are taxed at 3.7%, slightly higher than the grocery tax, and sometimes will include a few ingredients that you are less than excited about. For some people, a budget breakfast will make everything easier and a little cheaper. For this, you have two main options: cafes, which I will discuss in a minute, and supermarkets. Supermarkets generally have a giant case of breads and pastries, including croissants, mini pizzas, and often muffins. The discerning traveler can easily stop by Coop or Migros and pick up a delicious breakfast at a fraction of the cost. At a supermarket, you can also pick up iced coffees in the refrigerated case, fresh juice, local fruit, and even cereal and milk to enjoy in the hotel room.

31. CAFES

Cafes in Geneva are quite a phenomenon. If you are looking for a delicious breakfast or a nice place to take a quick break before seeing the sites, a café is right for you. Cafes usually offer a case of baked goods, similar to a patisserie, as well as the usual coffee, tea, and hot chocolate. You can usually pick up sandwiches as well and sometimes a few hot dishes prepared in the kitchen. Yuki Café offers a Japanese twist on traditional café offerings, while Cottage Café offers beautiful outdoor seating and a more classic café menu. For out-of-this-world espresso and brunch, try the Barista Lab in Plainpalais. Or do what I usually do and just start walking. One of the best cafes I have ever found was on a walk with my boyfriend through the Old Town. It was freezing cold, we picked the first place that we saw – and it was amazing. They had some of the creamiest, crunchiest chocolate eclairs that I have ever tasted. Unfortunately, I don't remember the name and have not been able to find it again, but maybe you'll be luckier.

32. BEST BARS

Like its cafes, Geneva's bars offer a great atmosphere to sit back, relax, and enjoy a few drinks. Although drinks in Geneva can be quite expensive, and most upscale hotels will have a well-reputed bar in the lobby, there are also a few more unique options for the intrepid traveler. My favorite, La Vere a Monique, is a self-proclaimed speakeasy with some of the most creative, delicious cocktails I have ever tried. Mr. Barber is another local bar with excellent cocktails and great vibes, although it is a slight bit more expensive. Finally, L'Atelier Cocktail Club has a more laid-back environment and is staffed by professional mixologists who really know their trade. Just like with Geneva's café scene, the best bars are often stumbled on by accident, so feel free to ignore my suggestions and just take a walk around Old Town in the evening. You could find something unique and lovely that even the locals don't know.

33. BEST BEERS

Switzerland is home to a number of beers and breweries, many of which are familiar to foreigners and locals alike. One of the most popular with locals is the hard-to-pronounce Feldschloesschen, as well as the more common Carlsberg and Heineken. Swiss beers are mostly pale lagers and, while they may not be as creative as the brews from other countries, are classic and good-quality across the board.

34. LOVELY LOCAL WINERIES

Geneva is renowned for its wines, as Lake Geneva is recognized as an excellent climate for wine production. If you have time for a day trip, a visit to a local winery like Cave de Geneve en Satigny, Domaine des Molards en Russin, or Domaine de Trois Etoiles en Satigny is sure to be a hit. Many vineyards also offer tours, hikes, and/or wine tasting: check out their websites for the most up-to-date information. If you don't have time or transportation to leave Geneva behind, have no fear. Just swing by Moevenpick Wines, where you have the opportunity to taste a wide range of local wines with no time limit or obligation to make a purchase. Le Verre en Cave

47

also offers fine wines as well as wine courses if you are looking for an educational element to your travels.

35. WATER: TAP OR BOTTLED?

Geneva has some of the best quality water in the world, whether you are buying a bottle or drinking directly from the tap. Most locals drink tap water, including me, and have reported no issues with it. You can usually get tap water in restaurants as well if you ask for it, which can save you a bit of money.

On the other hand, Switzerland does have particularly interesting bottled water, including both still and sparkling variations as well as flavored waters. Evian, the well-known bottled water brand consumed around the world, is produced right next to Geneva and draws upon Lake Geneva for its packaging. It may well be worth buying a bottle just for the fun of knowing that you are right next to the source.

36. UNIQUELY SWISS DRINKS

Apart from bottled water, Geneva boasts a range of delicious and unique non-alcoholic beverages. Perhaps the most famous, and strangest, is Rivella, a soft drink made from whey particles. This surprisingly tasty drink is quite popular for its flavor and dose of calcium with every sip. Schorle is another popular healthier soda option. Made of juice in a variety of flavors mixed with sparkling water, schorle is a popular drink for both children and adults. Finally, you simply must try a glass of local Swiss milk: it really does taste better, even when it comes in a bag in the supermarket.

37. UNIQUELY SWISS SNACKS

Switzerland also boasts some quite delicious snacks, which you can often pick up in your local grocery store. On the savory side, enjoy some Swiss potato chips, which usually come in three flavors: salt, paprika, and herb. The paprika chips are especially delicious, and whenever I leave Switzerland I find myself craving these flavorful crisps. Geneva also offers Pomme Bears, a puffed savory snack in the shape of teddy bears. These are also available in salt and paprika flavors and are quite addictive: I have been known to finish a bag by myself more than once.

For sweet snacks, make sure to try vermicelli, a uniquely Swiss dish made of chestnut noodles and usually topped with whipped cream. Small boxes are available in supermarkets, but for higher quality and fresher chestnut noodles, make sure to try a plate in a local restaurant. And give it time: the first time I ate vermicelli I was not a big fan, but by the second time I was in love.

38. VEGAN AND VEGETARIAN DELIGHTS

Geneva is slowly growing more and more aware of alternative diets, particularly in regards to vegetarians. Almost every restaurant will now offer a few vegetarian options, which are usually quite delicious. Vegan options are a bit rarer, but still can be found in a few restaurants, especially if you are willing to order a selection of side dishes and assemble your own meal. While Swiss food tends to include a lot of meat and dairy, international restaurants do a particularly good job of including vegan and vegetarian options.

If you are looking for a restaurant with a specifically vegan/vegetarian friendly menu, the first place you should go is Be Kind Café. With a range of vegan options, including delicious desserts, Be Kind Cafe is a hit with all of my vegan friends and is our first stop whenever they come to visit. The staff are particularly friendly and the food is both delicious and healthy. EnVie Vegan and Gateaux Sains Geneve are bakeries with some truly amazing vegan desserts that taste, in my opinion, even better than the non-vegan originals. For savory food, make sure to check out the Hamburger Foundation, which offers delicious vegan burgers as well as meat ones.

39. GLUTEN-FREE GOURMET

Just as Geneva is slowly catching on to vegetarian and vegan foods, it is also getting better about including gluten-free options on the menu. Again, many restaurants will have a few gluten-free options, although you will probably have to ask your waiter to confirm which dishes are gluten-free as they are not always marked. For specialty gluten-free cuisine, try

Mango Deck, which offers gluten-free international food for lunch and brunch (although they close for dinner). Be Kind Café also has numerous gluten-free options, as does Alive, a health food restaurant near Jardin Anglais. Both of these restaurants also offer gluten-full options, though, so make sure to check with your waiter before digging in.

40. RAW REVOLUTION

Raw food is a revolution that Geneva has not yet become particularly involved in. In most restaurants, raw foodies will mainly encounter salads. Don't fret, though, because Geneva does have some quite spectacular salads that are on wide offer. There are also a few specialty options. Two restaurants, Alive and Tartares & Co, provide some quite interesting raw options and are certainly worth a visit. Alive is a health food restaurant, so their raw options are focused on wholesomeness and taste, which can be appealing to many raw foodies. Tartares & Co, on the other hand, focuses on raw meats, which provides a uniquely culinary experience for fans of ceviche and, of course, tartar, but may not be a favorite for health-conscious raw foodies. With all this in mind, let's discuss the logistics of sitting down to dinner.

41. RESERVATIONS

In most upscale restaurants, and even in smaller restaurants that have limited seating, it is a good idea to make a reservation in advance. There are three ways to do this: the first is to visit the restaurant in person and put your name down. This is a good way to scope out the seating and menu before committing, but can be a little time consuming if the restaurant is on the other side of the city. The second is to call ahead. Most restaurants will have a phone number listed on their website where you can call and reserve a table. Most wait staff speak English well, but occasionally you will find someone whose English is basic or nonexistent. In these cases, it may be better to find an alternative way to reserve your spot. The third option is to reserve a table online. Most restaurants will have a small button on their website where you can fill in a brief questionnaire, choose your date and time, and book a table. This is usually the easiest option when it is available, as you can bypass any French language issues and save a bit of time.

Many less formal restaurants, such as pizza places, kebab shops, or casual international restaurants, do not require a reservation: this is usually clear if you stop by the restaurant. You can also call ahead to check if a reservation is needed if you are feeling unsure.

42. WILD WEST TABLE MANNERS

Alright, this title may be a little bit misleading. The Genevoise don't actually act like 1800s cowboys over dinner, but a few of their table traditions do come from some pretty fascinating, and a little wild-west style, origins. For instance, you should always keep both hands on the table while you are eating (don't rest a hand in your lap, for instance). This comes from the days when diners could point a gun at each other under the table with a free hand. Another Swiss tradition is to make and maintain eye contact while toasting, sometimes even spilling a little bit of your drink into the other diner's glass. This came about when people would occasionally poison each other's drinks over dinner: eye contact and mixing the drinks makes it more difficult to slip poison into someone else's glass.

A few other facets of Swiss table manners are also important, but have a less exciting backstory. Elbows should not be rested on the table, for instance. A clean plate represents enjoyment of the meal. Mouth noises are discouraged. And of course, leave your gun and poison at home for a pleasant dining experience.

43. GETTING AROUND THE CITY

You will need some way to get between the different restaurants that you're looking forward to visiting, right? Luckily, Geneva has a fantastic public transportation system. There is a series of buses, as well as an extensive tram network, that will take you just about anywhere you want to go within the city. You can purchase tickets for the Geneva Public Transport, or TPG (from the French name), on the TPG app, which can be downloaded for free from the app store, or at any of the small machines present at almost every bus or tram stop. If you are a senior, child, or student, you can purchase tickets at half the price: just be sure to select this option when purchasing your ticket and have an identity card on hand in case you are checked.

Bus and tram times and routes can be viewed on the TPG app, on small maps located in each bus, or simply on Google Maps. Public transportation is usually punctual, clean, and pleasant in Geneva, and is an excellent way to travel. For shorter distances, walking is also a perfect way to get around, as Geneva is very pedestrian friendly.

44. WHERE TO STAY

Many tourists choose to stay in the Old Town, a central part of Geneva. This is an excellent choice, as this part of Geneva is not only beautiful and historic, but is also quite close to most popular sites and attractions. It is not the only choice, though. For travelers looking to go a bit off the beaten path, Thonex is an attractive choice. There, you will be surrounded by local crowds and can find accommodations and food at a more reasonable price. What's not to love about that? For travelers who are particularly excited about the international parts of Geneva, I recommend staying near Nations. This neighborhood is popular with locals who moved to Geneva from around the world because of its delicious food and proximity to international organizations like the United Nations. Finally, Champel is a lovely, historic neighborhood about 30 minutes from the center of Geneva on public transportation. This neighborhood is popular with students and young people and has a great vibe.

45. ESSENTIAL PHRASES

Almost everyone in Geneva speaks excellent English (and sometimes German, Spanish, Italian, or any number of other languages as well). If you are excited to practice French, though, here are a few phrases that will be particularly useful on your travels.

Good morning – Bonjour
Thank you – Merci
Thank you very much – Merci beaucoup
You're welcome – De rien
Excuse me – Excusez-moi
Please – S'il vous plait

Goodbye – Au revoir (not adieu, adieu means that you don't plan to see someone again until after you are both dead)

I would like… – Je voudrais…

A table for (two) please – Une table pour (deux) s'il vous plait

Where is…? -- Ou est…?

46. TRAIN STATION TREATS

The Cornavin train station is often the last (or first) place that visitors see when they arrive in Geneva. It is also the place I usually arrive back to the city after visiting another part of Switzerland, and I am usually starving. Don't worry: the train station offers some quite delicious, cheap, and quick food. Although the restaurants there change frequently, you can always count on a few coffee shops, a bakery or two, a few small grocery stores, and one or two restaurants serving hot food. I recommend picking up a few snacks before you head off on your next adventure – the train station usually also offers a chocolate shop where you can stock up before heading out.

47. AIRPORT EATS

If you don't arrive and leave from Cornavin, you probably are coming in and out of Geneva's international airport. Although airports are not usually known for exciting food, Geneva's airport actually offers some pretty good food for a quick bite – and one truly spectacular restaurant for a final hurrah before you fly home. Il Forno, Little Coffee Shop, and Pasta Box all offer tasty fresh food that you can grab before you take off. If you have a bit more time and money, Le Chef is a sophisticated restaurant with a range of dining rooms to choose based on your mood and a unique, local menu. Le Chef is consistently ranked as one of the best restaurants in Geneva, and you can enjoy it on your way to the runway.

48. SOUVENIR SWEETS

Before you pack up and head to the airport or train station, be sure to pick up a few souvenir foods to take home to your family and friends. Swiss chocolate is always an excellent choice and can be picked up either at a grocery store, for a cheaper option, or at specialty shops like Laederach for a more sophisticated experience. You can also pick up a few of the iconic Toblerones, although these are not commonly eaten in Switzerland and you might get a few funny looks if you purchase one. Just smile and wave.

If you're traveling to a closer destination, I recommend picking up a few pastries from the local patisserie for special people back home. Although they can get a little squished during travel, your family and friends will certainly appreciate the delicious flavors – as long as you can hold off eating them yourself until you get home.

For longer journeys, choose a Kagi bar instead. These chocolate-filled wafers are iconic within Switzerland and are much beloved by schoolchildren itching to spend their allowance and by adults craving a sweet treat alike.

49. EMBRACING THE UNEXPECTED

Are you getting excited? Are you starting to feel hungry? I certainly am. I have listed here a few of my personal favorite restaurants and culinary experiences that I truly believe you will love as much as I do. Any traveler or local will know, though, that not everything goes according to plan. And that's perfect! Some of my best food memories in Geneva, from my first date with my boyfriend to amazing coffee shops and picturesque picnics, happened completely by accident. So, embrace the unexpected. Stop, not just to smell the flowers, but also to smell the fresh coffee wafting out of a tiny corner café. Try the vermicelli, even if you've never heard of it before, because you might love it. Wander the streets and find your own best restaurants, best desserts, and best memories. And then tell me about it, because I want to try your favorite restaurant, too!

50. SO, WHAT ARE YOU WAITING FOR?

I'm sitting here in front of my computer, telling you all the things to love about eating like a local in Geneva, but I won't be here for long. In a few minutes, I'll shut my laptop and head out for dinner. I think I'll have a falafel wrap from Parfums de Beyrouth, then maybe split a milkshake over at Black Tap. Do you want to come?

I hope that, in reading this book, you'll have gotten a small taste of how wonderful Geneva really is. So, are you ready to sample it for yourself? Are you ready to dip a chunk of crusty bread into a cauldron of bubbling fondue? Are you ready to dig in to a meal built on local, seasonal flavors? Are you ready to peer over the edge of an ice cream cart, deciding which ice cream you want to try today? Come on, then! What are you waiting for?

OTHER RESOURCES:

For more general information about visiting Geneva, check out the Geneva Tourism website:
https://www.geneve.com/en/

For public transportation maps, schedules, and prices, see the TPG's official website:
https://www.tpg.ch/en

For ordering food in, try:
https://www.just-eat.ch/en/

TASTE OF THE SEASONS

Plainpalais Farmer's Market
Geneva
Open Tuesday, Thursday, and Sunday

Orchard St-Loup
Versoix

Cueillettes de Landecy
Meyrin

La Cave de Geneve
Satigny

READ OTHER BOOKS BY CZYK PUBLISHING

Eat Like a Local United States Cities & Towns

Eat Like a Local United States

Eat Like a Local- Oklahoma: Oklahoma Food Guide

Eat Like a Local- North Carolina: North Carolina Food Guide

Eat Like a Local- New York City: New York City Food Guide

Children's Book: Charlie the Cavalier Travels the World by Lisa Rusczyk

Eat Like a Local

Follow *Eat Like a Local on* Amazon.
Join our mailing list for new books

http://bit.ly/EatLikeaLocalbooks

CZYKPublishing.com

Made in the USA
Las Vegas, NV
03 September 2023

77013170R00046